Praise for
Truth Be Told
The Incident at Bravo Checkpoint

"Author Rex Barton writes action books based on his own experiences. In Truth Be Told he writes of post-WWII tension in militarily divided Berlin. The tale that he recounts fits right into a genre that fans of W. E. B. Griffin eagerly seek!"
- R. Paul Gookins, U.S. Veteran

"A true story told first-hand by the author, exceptionally gripping and poignant. An insightful documentary that puts a spotlight back on the facts of this tragic incident at Bravo Checkpoint."
- Bruce J. Tapper, Ph.D.

"Praise to the author for revealing his truth about this atrocity he lived through, detailing the era and events during one of the darkest periods of time in the history of humanity."
- George Mathew, MD, Ph.D.

"Rex Barton has the ability to put you there on the scene with a clear and precise recantation… woven with details of fact…including the state of mind of those involved. Not only all that, but he astoundingly remembers what was for lunch that day in 1965! Every time I read one of his books, I learn something new."
- Jeffrey L. Sickler, Avid Reader

TRUTH BE TOLD

THE INCIDENT AT BRAVO CHECKPOINT

Rex Barton

ISBN 978-1-957220-93-2 (paperback)
ISBN 978-1-957220-94-9 (digital)

Copyright Rex Barton

All rights reserved. No part of this publication may be reproduced, distributed, Or transmitted in any form or by any means, including photocopying, recording, or other electronic or mechanical methods without the prior written permission of the publisher. For permission requests, solicit the publisher via the address below.

Hawk Tales Publishing, LLC
www.HawkTalesPublishing.com

Printed in the United States of America

DEDICATIONS

I dedicate *Truth Be Told - The Incident at Bravo Checkpoint* to all those who have served in the armed forces of the United States of America. Thank you for your service.

Resources:

- Veterans Crisis Line: 1-800-273-8255 and Press 1
- National Suicide Prevention Lifeline: 1-800-273-8255
- White House VA Hotline: 1-855-948-2311
- Mental Health Hotline: 844-395-1271

To my wife, Antionette, who spends many lonely nights feeling like an author's widow as I type away in my office. Thank you for believing in me.

A special thank you to Jodi Pappas for her countless hours researching, consulting, and editing this important historical and resourceful book.

"For God so loved the world that he gave his one and only Son, that whoever believes in him shall not perish but have eternal life." (John 3:16) NIV

Rex Barton was born June 24, 1944, in Santa Barbara, California, USA. Raised by his loving grandparents on a walnut farm in Ventura, California, he learned to be an avid horseman and care for all animals big and small, from an elephant to a hummingbird.

In the summer of 1962, he joined the United States Army and completed his basic and military occupational specialty (MOS) training at Fort Ord Army post on Monterey Bay in California. Subsequently, he was stationed in Berlin, Germany, a cold war zone, and assigned to the 287th Military Police Company as a Military Policeman (MP) for almost five years. The duties were to guard military and civilian train passengers through dangerous zones, conduct routine patrols in the sectors, boat patrol Wannsee Lake and surrounding waterways, and assist with working on cases in the Criminal Investigation Division (CID). His stories are captivating and intense.

In March 1967, Rex became a Deputy Sheriff/Deputy Coroner with the Santa Barbara County Sheriff's Department where he served over seven years until he retired in 1974 due to a service-related disability. He worked in numerous divisions, including patrol, detention, courts/civil, juvenile, and investigations. After relocating

Rex Barton

to the Channel Island area near Ventura, Rex became a licensed, independent Mortgage Broker/Realtor for many years.

In 2013, Rex moved with his wife to the Pacific Northwest where he enjoys writing novels in various genres.

Only the dead have seen the end of war. – Plato

An eyewitness account of a couple shot in cold blood by East German border guards during the Cold War. A true story told by the military police boat commander and the first to arrive at the scene.

The day occurred more than a half-century ago on the Teltow Canal at Bravo Checkpoint in Berlin, Germany. It was Tuesday, June 15th, 1965. Still hidden in the bloodbath of that day is the truth.

The soviet controlled German Democratic Republic (GDR) generated outrageous lies about the incident and the victims. News reports circulated the false narratives worldwide. The families of Hermann Dobler and Elke Martens deserve to know what happened and to have the record set straight.

This memoir details the author's eyewitness account of the tragic day to the best of his recollection. In addition, he shares some of his personal military experiences along the way.

Preface

I was serving as the U.S. Army Military Police (MP) Boat Patrol Commander in Berlin, Germany, on June 15, 1965, when we arrived on the scene of an active shooting. Hans was the helmsman and owner of the boat, Private First Class (PFC) Rudy was my second in command, a young, new Military Policeman (MP) from Arizona. It was our duty and obligation to protect both military and civilian lives on the lakes and canals in West Berlin.

As we approached, our patrol boat took on direct fire from the East German guard tower. With my rifle raised I looked through the scope and slightly leaned my head to the right when suddenly a bullet grazed the left side of my head above my ear. I had been nearly killed by the same East German guard that had just shot Herman Dobler and Elke Martens. We experienced the malignity of the guards and witnessed the aftermath of the ruthless shootings of the victims.

People feared that Bravo Checkpoint was under attack. An intense military build-up ensued on either side of the Teltow Canal where the incident occurred. There were U.S. military tanks and a company of U.S. infantry faced off against Russian tanks and Russian/East German soldiers. I stood on the West German embankment in the middle of the standoff with the shooting victims, one rookie PFC and one helmsman. I watched as the guns and tanks from both sides were all directed towards us.

Rex Barton

More than twenty years after the killings, that same guard who shot the victims was finally found guilty of murder and imprisoned. Fifty-five years after this incident at Bravo Checkpoint, it is still hidden in the United States military archives. Many of the battles and stand-offs that occurred were never reported by the military for reasons of security, or the severity of the situation, or whether American lives were lost.

Prologue

The terrifying incident happened to a West Berlin businessman named Hermann Dobler and a young woman who was with him, presumably Elke Martens. It was June 15, 1965, and the two had a picnic basket with them for a boat ride around Wannsee Lake and canals. Many other boats were on the water that beautiful day, including our U.S. Army Military Police patrol boat.

My team and I responded to the scene that day as it was unfolding. Hours later, I had written in my police report that the couple had navigated their boat along the west side of Teltow Canal, possibly looking for a place to have their picnic. Little did they know that they were in the presence of evil. Two East German (Volkspolizit) VoPo guards stationed inside the guard tower above were watching them.

The families of these victims and the world at large deserve to know the truth about what happened to this couple. I was there, and I have carried the memory of them in my heart for over 55 years, yet I never knew their names until recently when I was researching for my autobiography. Official documents and newspapers have reported inaccuracies. It is essential to understand the history of my military career and experiences prior to the horrific event. This is my first-hand account of an unarmed couple who were under fire with nowhere to hide. It is a day seared into my heart. It is time the *Truth Be Told*.

For the Victims:

Elke Martens and Hermann Dobler

This story began before I was even born. Prior to the start of World War II in 1939, European history reported that there were more than 9.5 million Jewish people living throughout all of Europe. After World War II ended in 1945, Adolf Hitler's Third Reich Nazi Party and dreaded SS troops (Schutzstaffel - elite corps), had killed 6 million Jews.

It was as early as 1922 that Hitler provided clues regarding his ambitions to commit mass genocide. Annihilation of all Jews was one of his foremost tasks, and he would never give up until they were erased from civilization. He had ordered the Jews and any political detainees to be executed.

Hitler even ordered falsely accused political prisoners to be killed as well as many other innocent people, including babies, children, and prisoners of war. It didn't matter if they were German, Jewish, or a foreigner of any kind, the Nazis had no regard for human life. Most of the people were innocent of crimes, except for a few so-called criminals that had stolen food attempting to feed their starving families. Hitler started World War II, but he never gave losing the war or dying himself a second thought. He lost the war and he committed suicide in a bunker.

Many books have been written about the concentration camps and the brave people who helped others. Including stories about the horrible camps with names such as Auschwitz concentration camp, Belzec extermination camp, Bergen-Belsen concentration camp, Buchenwald concentration camp, Chelmno extermination camp, Dachau concentration camp, Ebensee concentration camp, and Flossenburg concentration camp.

In these places, they killed Jews, Americans, English, and French prisoners of war. The Nazis called this barbaric behavior "Endlosung" or in English, "answer to the Jewish question."

The Cold War Era began in 1945 and lasted until 1991. After World War II, Germany was separated. East Germany was occupied by the Soviet Union, a communist state. West Germany was occupied by the United States, Great Britain, and France, a capitalist democracy.

The city of Berlin, located in the Soviet zone 200 miles inside East Germany, was similarly divided. In 1965, it was an occupied city like none other. It was a city within a city. Berlin was comprised of sectors, and those sectors or boundaries included Russia, France, England, and America.

Map of Germany and Berlin Sectors

There were only four ways out of Berlin. One was to fly out of Tempelhof Air Force Base. The second and third were to either drive out or ride the train from Bravo Checkpoint to West Germany. The fourth, and least preferred, was to be shot and killed by the East German police kill squads.

It was a time in history of intense turmoil, horror, disbelief, and sadness. There were many deaths and grieving families being torn apart between East and West Berlin.

The Soviet communist government wanted to halt American capitalism from infiltrating their communism. On August 13, 1961, the construction of a wall began to prevent East German refugees from fleeing to West Germany. While the wall was being built, the military infantry and armored divisions of the communist armies were shoulder to shoulder, surrounding Berlin to stop anyone from crossing in either direction, even if that meant death.

The communist armies frequently used the rivers, lakes, and old wells to bury, dump, and hide dead bodies, sinking them with rocks. In Berlin, near the Bravo Checkpoint, rotting cadavers would work loose from the rocks and float up to the top where they could be spotted on the East German side of the canals and Wannsee Lake. Many Military Policemen (MPs), like myself, were tasked with pulling the decomposing corpses from the water when they were reported, about 1-2 bodies per month. Often, they were so decomposed that they would disintegrate all over me as I tried to lift them out of the water.

Circled is Checkpoint Bravo and Wannsee area

The U.S. Army

It was December 1962 when I joined the United States Army. I had just turned 18, and two weeks after graduation, I was riding on a Greyhound bus headed to Los Angeles for my physicals. My dream was to work hard and become an officer in the Army. From Los Angeles, I was sent by bus to Fort Ord, California to the United States Army post on Monterey Bay for my basic training. Next, I completed eight weeks of Military Occupation Specialty (MOS) training.

After my MOS graduation, I was called into the company commander's office to find out my new duty station. The commander told me that somehow my orders read Berlin, Germany.

"I'm not sure how this order came down for you private, because the rest of the battalion is scheduled for South Korea duty," the commander stated. "You must have some pull from somewhere if your orders have you going to Berlin. Listen to me private, it is dangerous over there in Germany, so I suggest you stay on high alert. One more thing, keep your head down and good luck over there."

Two days later, I was looking out the window of a TWA jet plane bound for New York City. My friend William Vandermark, the Undersheriff of the Santa Barbara Sheriff's Department, stayed true to his word. He had helped me get into his old duty station, the 287th Military Police Company in Berlin, Germany.

Military Police and Berlin Patches

Berlin Special Troops Patch

I flew alone from Los Angeles to New York and landed during one of the coldest winters on record, I was totally unprepared. My duffle bag was a little light for the conditions as I was never issued any winter clothing. Maybe having some essential items like a Parka and winter gloves could have helped prevent me from freezing. I had already learned not to put my frozen hands under cold water, feeling that excruciating pain took one lesson to never do that again. From there, I took a bus to Fort Dix Military Base in New Jersey, where I finally received proper clothing to survive the elements.

After two long weeks of being frozen half to death in New Jersey, this southern California surfer was driven to the debarkation port. I marched onto a big troop transportation ship called the USS *Patch*. *Funny name for a ship*, I thought to myself.

The day finally came when I walked down the gangplank at Bremerhaven Seaport in West Germany. From there, I was taken by a military bus to the train station and headed for my new duty station in Berlin.

The USS *Patch* 1962

One day while we were out at sea, one of the Navy personnel came around and told our entire group of 100 soldiers holed up down below that the ship was famous for having sunk three times during World War II. Well, that was not very comforting to know. *Surely, they jested*.

From my perspective, being on this ship was a grave mistake, but I had no influence on the Captain about turning it around. Being cooped up for two weeks at the bottom of the ship was certainly not vacation time. It bordered on inhumane conditions. There were hammock-like hanging beds on top of one another that made sleeping uncomfortable. The smells and odors from all the people living under close quarters was awful and no access to look out a window. At the bottom of the ship, where we were put, was the ship's engine compartment, a small cafeteria, toilets, and showers.

The USS General Alexander M. Patch Troop Ship

One day I left the dreaded hole and made my way up two flights of stairs to a porthole window. The military was not supposed to be where I was, but the change of scenery and a lookout of a window was well worth the ass-chewing, if any. *Would they really put me in the Brig?* I wondered. As far as I was concerned, I was already living there.

Since leaving the Port of New York a couple weeks ago, I believed the Captain had made a wrong turn, and we were now in Alaska. Out of the porthole to my utter surprise and shock were incredibly huge icebergs littering the ocean everywhere. Those icebergs seemed to be as big as our ship itself. One such iceberg was big enough to have sunk the Titanic.

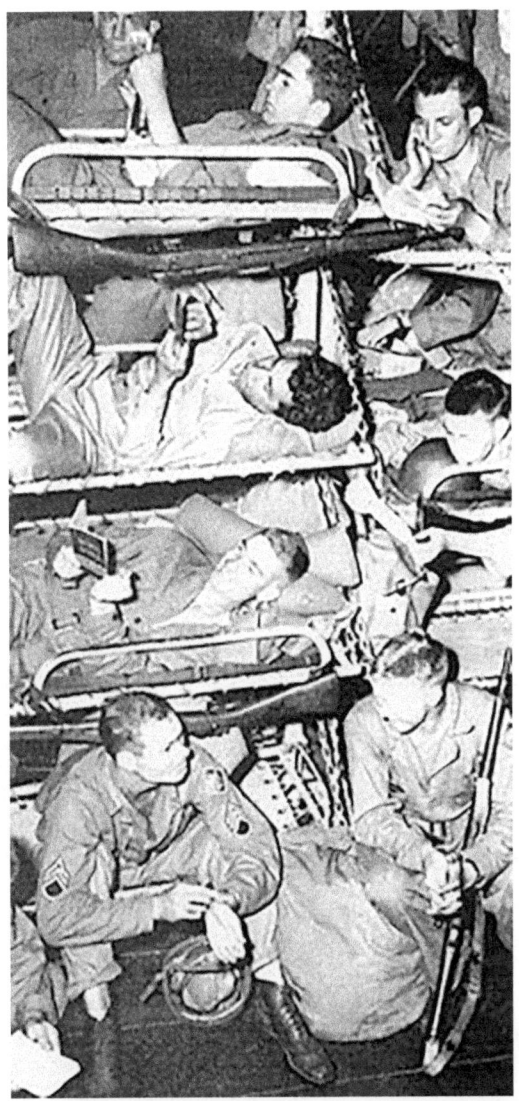

Troops in the bottom of the USS *Patch*

I was wrong. We were not in Alaska. What I was looking at was the frozen Atlantic icebergs, which return most winter months near Germany.

The Train to Berlin

When boarding the West German train to Berlin, two American MPs were there checking military orders and civilian passports. The MP train duty was born out of necessity because frequently while going through the demilitarized zone (DMZ) checkpoints, the East German VoPo guards would take civilians off the train and beat them. Once the MPs were stationed on the train, that type of violent behavior ended, only to be replaced by the guards' verbal abuse and threats.

U.S. Army Military Police Corps Medal

The MPs told me not to worry and, above all, stay in my assigned seat to avoid enemy problems. My facial expression of confusion must have said it all. I thought, *why can't I leave my seat? Enemy, what enemy?* I was not the only American military person on the train, but I felt very much alone at this moment. It was then I remembered what my MOS commander had told me, *"Keep your head down and good luck over there."*

It wasn't long after boarding the train and finding my assigned seat, that we began our journey to Berlin. The train wound its way through the beautiful countryside of West Germany with its quaint little towns. Then we stopped at an area called 'The Zone,' which is Communist East Germany. This is the DMZ which separates East and West Germany en route to Berlin. The Zone is where East German guards board the trains and check all passengers for proper documentation. This is the time they often antagonize the passengers.

Before stopping, all the people on the train were told to stay in their seats until we passed by the blockades. In the Army, when you are advised not to leave your position under any circumstances, except to go to the bathroom, you follow orders. But I wondered if I should be armed or something considering I was face to face with the enemy at two border crossings. Going through the DMZ and meeting the VoPo guards face-to-face was unsettling and disturbing.

The train came to a complete stop while VoPo guards walked all around it, looked underneath, and walked up and down the aisles. The guards had cold, blank stares and smelled filthy from lack of hygiene. They carried numerous weapons and wore wool uniforms and coats with square fur hats. After a complete inspection of the train and checking all people for identification, we were ready to start moving again. I thought to myself, *I have just met the enemy and survived. What's next?*

Through the DMZ, we continued until we reached the East-West Berlin border crossing. There we went through another border inspection, a recount of the people, and a check of all identification. After that little intermission, we moved on again. We crossed over the Avus bridge and I was now in West Berlin.

Finally, a name I remember seeing on my orders. *Berlin really does exist,* I thought. From there, I was given additional paperwork from another MP. I handed the paperwork to a taxi driver who then drove me to the front gate of the 287th Military Police Company.

The 287th Military Police Company

After arriving, I was given two days to adjust to my new home, learn the base boundaries, and read stacks of paperwork about all the dos and don'ts of military life in Berlin. I settled into my surroundings and got to work.

Rex in uniform at the 287th Military Policy Company

MP Booking Desk Assignment

As a Military Policeman (MP) my first assignment was the booking desk. I booked American soldiers who couldn't hold their liquor and were involved in bar fights. Other bookings included burglaries and many other fine manners of uncontrolled misconduct, requiring discipline.

I remember one incident where a taxi-cab driver drove up to our office honking his horn frantically. In the back seat was a woman about to give birth. Her water had broke and she was screaming bloody murder. I assisted my desk sergeant in delivering a very large baby boy! I remember putting a paperclip on the baby's umbilical cord and then putting the baby on the woman's chest. I wasn't scared at the time, but shortly after that, I started shaking. Delivering babies was never taught in school. This was just good old on the job training.

Three months later, I was reassigned to handle the MP Train detail. I remembered the train experience very well.

MP Train Detail Assignment

Working as an MP on the train, I learned all about the DMZ first-hand. Once again, I was vividly reminded how the VoPo guards behaved like a bunch of bullies as they constantly picked on the passengers. My job as an MP was to provide safety and protection for the passengers and military personnel traveling between Berlin and West Germany. My orders were to not let the VoPo guards take advantage of the people in my care or allow them to make attempts to remove anyone from the train. Many VoPo guards took great pleasure and seemed to enjoy harassing the Americans as well as other passengers.

I learned early on how much the VoPo guards valued a pack of American cigarettes. I used this as leverage. I would exchange a pack of cigarettes with the VoPo guards for their cooperation, efficient passenger checks, and easy passage through the zones.

The train ride was an overnight trip from Bremerhaven to West Berlin, with no beds. There were only a few bathrooms, and you had to be willing to stand for an hour waiting to use one. My job description never changed. Safely help bring both military personnel and civilians from the Port City of Bremerhaven to Berlin and back again.

During some of the physical searches on the train, escalating voices between the VoPo guards and American MPs could be heard. Sometimes even to the point where threats and shouting rang out into thin air.

On occasion, the VoPo guards threatened innocent people with violence or even death with their guns drawn. It never failed that once I pulled my .45-semi-auto sidearm and pointed it directly at the lead officer, they would back down and withdraw.

I learned soon enough just how cowardly the VoPo guards were. As if they were at target practice, they would shoot and kill or wound innocent men, women, and children as they attempted to flee East Berlin. As the wall went up, more and more people attempted to escape the horrors of living in East Berlin. People were starving, had no jobs or money, families were divided, and risking death seemed to be the only choice some people had to try and survive.

One of the problems was the Russians, they never liked the peace accord. Most of the VoPo guards were Russian-trained police or ex-German military. The Russians wanted all of Berlin, both East and West, all to themselves.

MP Routine Patrol Assignment

After three months of train detail witnessing the brutality of East German border guards and having to draw my .45-semi-auto weapon on occasion, I was given the opportunity for routine patrol duties throughout all the Berlin sectors. All except East Berlin, which was held by Russia.

On June 26, 1963, President John F. Kennedy came to West Berlin to speak with the people. I was assigned to protect the President as part of his honor guard security detail. To this day, I consider it an honor. During his speech, there was an enormous crowd with thousands of people who came out to see and hear the American President.

MP Rex standing on duty as John F. Kennedy's Special Honor Guard

In the picture, I am the MP in uniform standing in front of the platform wearing the white hat and white gloves. Sadly, President

wrong turn could cost you imprisonment in an East German prison camp, or worse yet, death in Prague, Czechia. I knew somehow, I had missed the proper turn, but how could anyone know when everything is snow-covered including most of the roadway? Nothing looked familiar any longer and I realized I was in East Germany. I was now twenty minutes late for work. Stopping was not an option, so I kept my foot on the pedal, put my emergency brake on, and turned the wheel, putting me into a slow sliding 180 degree turn around. Letting go of the emergency brake at the right time was my only hope of not ending up crashed and hidden out of sight in a snowbank. I got lucky this time and put the gas pedal to the floor with tires spinning and made up at least fifteen minutes of time when I finally reached the right fork in the road and got back on track to Berlin. That was a terrifying mistake.

Wannsee Lake stretched for miles with little tributaries and always the invisible lines in the water separating East and West. At the end of a beautiful, sloping grass lawn was a long, sandy beach. In the middle of this melody of beauty was a boat dock; our MP boat was moored to the dock all year round when not in use for duty patrol.

There were miles of beautiful homes with stunning green lawns that seemingly ran like waterfalls to the lake's edge. The beauty of the trees and sandy shores disguised the deadliness of the place.

The Wannsee Lake area was so dangerous because of the invisible line, a line that runs right down the middle of the water. That's right, only an invisible line in the water separated East and West Berlin, not a wall like Charlie Checkpoint. Signage was posted in specific areas warning people not to enter. The channel had been used as an escape route for refugees trying to flee East Germany. If any refugees even managed to make it this far down, the canal had hidden dangers lurking from above for those not familiar with East German tower guards.

Many refugees from East Germany would try to swim across the 30 to 40-foot width of the cold Teltow Canal in search of freedom in

The Visiting Generals

It was a frigid winter day in December 1964. My company commander told me that our patrol boat was to accompany four visiting generals from other Command Posts in Germany while they go bird hunting, out of season, of course. They wanted to go down close to one of the canals that shared the same problem as the Teltow. A small islet protected the canal opening and was the main encampment for a few VoPo guards. Frequently, we would run into one or two VoPo patrol boats when cruising by. Sometimes they would try and sneak around the islet to come up behind us. They could never catch us by surprise. We always expected shenanigans from the VoPo guards because we were passing so close to their turf. After trying to sneak up on us, we were ready for them and maneuvered the patrol boat around to end up nose to nose. When that happened, they would make a hasty exit backward and disappear behind the islet again.

Afterward, we would turn around and continue our patrol duties. It could have been dangerous because the VoPo guards transported .50 cal. DShK machine guns on their bows.

At that time in 1964, we only had .45 Auto pistol sidearms. Our military never thought the VoPo guards were much of a threat, even though refugee shootings were on the rise. As usual, we remained outgunned. Not exactly a fair fight if we ever had to engage the enemy.

While preparing to leave, I gave the four visiting generals a warning of possible problems in some regions of the lakes and off-limit areas in other places. They just scoffed at me with remarks.

"Don't worry about us, sonny," said one general.

Another general laughed out loud at his remark.

"We have more rights to be here than they do," a third general commented.

In other words, no one was going to break-up their duck hunting party. Although they were loud and boisterous, we prepared them with the latest in winter gear for being on an icy lake and issued them shotguns. It was a rather calm day on the frigid waters with no wind.

It only took a few minutes for me to prepare the 16-foot motorized boat for the generals to use. Besides the cold weather, Wannsee Lake had at least a half-inch of ice covering it. Small boats such as the skiff the generals were using weren't made for cutting ice. Hans had previously made an aluminum bow guard cover to stop the ice from sinking the little boat. The coffee the generals had before addressing us that morning had to be spiked. Their heavy alcohol breath nearly knocked me over. It didn't take a fool to figure out that a cold day, plus alcohol, and not paying attention was a disaster waiting to happen.

The four generals took the lead as they shoved off ahead of our patrol boat. They were evenly seated one behind the other with the last manhandling the motorized tiller. We stayed approximately seventy-five yards behind the skiff. That was a safe distance to remain behind because I didn't feel like getting shot today.

The generals had fired off a couple of shotgun blasts that missed every flying duck. All we heard on the MP boat was shotgun blasts and then loud cursing when they missed. It could be that having hot toddies that early in the morning saved the lives of many ducks. I thank God that we weren't at war.

Suddenly, without warning or provocation, a VoPo boat came around the islet at full speed and headed straight towards the generals' little skiff. As soon as I saw the bow of the VoPo boat rounding the islet, I immediately pushed the throttle full forward to make up the distance between our two boats.

The generals were not prepared for what happened next. For one thing, no one was even paying attention to the front line of the boat. I tried to shout to them, but they wouldn't or couldn't hear me. I think in retrospect, the VoPo guards may have overheard the generals yelling and their snide remarks and obviously all the shotgun blasts. They must have gotten worried they were in the general's line of fire.

At any rate, the VoPo guards took a full run at the generals and, at the last moment, slipped right by their skiff, leaving only a couple of feet before they turned sharply again between our patrol boat and the islet. As they were speeding away, they even fired a few shots into the air. What usually happens in these cases is the smaller boat loses, and the occupants are thrown overboard into the water. That was precisely what happened right in front of me.

All four generals were tossed into the icy cold water, losing more than their hats. All four shotguns sank to the bottom. If you are aware of the military #1 code, it is a soldier (including generals) shalt not lose your weapon under any circumstance.

The boat was of little use to the generals as it was upside down now. All four were quickly losing the battle to hypothermia. When we came alongside their boat, my only choice was to remove my coat and shoes and jump into the frigid water. One by one, I grabbed each general from behind pushed them toward Rudy and Hans while they pulled them up onto our MP boat. With the help of my two deckhands, they pulled each one up into the boat as I pushed from in the water.

Once all four generals were safe aboard the patrol boat, my crew covered each of them with blankets. I hoisted myself out of the water and wrapped a blanket around me as well. I ordered one of my partners to leave the skiff and turn our boat around to get us back to our dock fast.

We radioed headquarters and requested to have help standing by and to call the company commander and advise him of our situation. It took approximately fifteen minutes to reach our dock. After we arrived, no less than a dozen people were standing by ready to administer first aid. Other than being frozen cold, tired, and embarrassed, all four generals thanked us for our service and for saving their lives.

Not long after this incident, the generals had ordered us M14 rifles to assist in our protection while on duty. We had only been asking headquarters for six months for some weaponry. I guess we should have invited the generals to go hunting last December. Requisitions such as more firepower got answered in strange ways. Even though the M14s were a welcomed improvement, maybe the powers that be thought we were faster shooters, thus we never had to worry about more massive guns.

The Summers

With winter's thaw came bright warm days. What a welcome that was to switch from our winter uniforms to summer short-sleeve fatigues. We spent our time going up and down Wannsee Lake helping people back to shore who tried to swim out too far, towing broken-down boats, and checking all the canals.

At times we even managed to do a little water-skiing during lunch breaks or give some visiting military families tours on our boat of Wannsee Lake. Everything was seemingly normal for this time of year, according to Hoyle. Eighty-degree days and sunny.

The helmsman of our patrol boat, Hans, was born and raised in Germany. He was a short man, at 5'5" and was starting to bald. There had to be more to his background than the few German Marks that our military paid him for the use of himself and his 26-foot boat. He was always worried about everything unimportant. Hans never talked about the war. In fact, he didn't talk much at all. In the early morning, it was 'Guten Morgen' (Good morning) or in the afternoon, 'Guten Tag' (Good afternoon). Only when I was driving his boat did I hear oblique words in German under his breath. It didn't take long for him to realize how well I understood and communicated in German, not that it stopped him from cussing. That was just Hans. Like him or not, he was the man with the boat that steered us through many a dangerous moment in my history while in Berlin.

Hans lived in one of the prestigious shoreline homes of Wannsee Lake most of his adult life. To this day, I could not tell you how he gained so much after the end of the war. Most Germans were impoverished and still struggling to make ends meet, even though in West Berlin Capitalism was doing very well. The Wannsee Villa, once Hitler's lake home, was now the officer's club and the 287th MP Boat Patrol Headquarters.

The Wannsee Villa - Hilter's former home
The 287th MP Boat Headquarters and Officers
club is located at the bottom right

The Incident at Bravo Checkpoint

The day began like any other summer day. It was Tuesday, June 15th, 1965, only nine days before my 21st birthday. I was already married to a lovely German woman and we had a 17-day-old infant daughter at home. This day, before it ended, would take all I had to live through. America, the military, and even the President of the United States had no idea how close we came to war. It was an incident that had a tremendous impact on me. My upbringing, my grandparents, even my absent mother, came into play this day. Most of all, it was my faith in God.

Teltow Canal and the East German VoPo guard
tower opposite Bravo Checkpoint

"Guten Morgen." (Good morning.) Hans said to me at 0700 hrs. on June 15, 1965.

"Guten Morgen Herr Hans. Wie Geht es dir?" (Good morning, Hans. How are you?) I asked.

"Sehr Gut. Danke." (Very good, thanks.) Hans replied.

"Bist du bereit fur weiterer heiber tag?" (Are you ready for another hot day?)

"Jawohl Mein Herr." (Yes, sir.) Hans answered.

I opened the office to retrieve our logs and asked Hans if the coffee was ready yet.

"Ja Jawohl. Sahne und Zucker?" (Yes, you bet. Cream and sugar?) Hans inquired.

"Ja Danke, Hans." (Yes, thank you, Hans.)

After collecting what we needed to take with us this morning, Hans went down to get the boat ready while Rudy and I finished up. Rudy worked on patrol in Arizona for one year before transferring to our boat patrol. We used to talk a lot about going to flight school in Arizona. Learning to pilot was a dream we both had.

Hans had the boat warmed up when Rudy and I boarded with our coffees and clipboards in hand. As I went over the schedule with

Hans and the points of interest that I wanted to check this morning, Rudy untied our vessel, and Hans put our maiden in gear. We left our dock slowly, and Hans guided her in a long and slow right turn. It was time to visit the islet where the generals went overboard this past winter.

We were notified earlier that the VoPo guards had been target practicing at homes in the American sector early this morning and at boats passing by the invisible line in the water, denoting the American and East German boundaries. The military took exception to this careless activity and Capt. D. asked me to have a little talk with the border guards. Yes sir, I will make it known, sir. Their target practice could have killed innocent people, damaged property, and it needed to stop today.

I told Hans I would take over control of the patrol boat. He sat down inside. We didn't hear shouts of laughter from the VoPo guards until we rounded the bend, having crossed the invisible line. Several VoPo guards were hanging around in their boat when suddenly they saw us coming towards them. Their cups went up in the air, and the coffee inside of them went flying everywhere.

"Vas ist Los comrades?" (What's up friends?) I shouted in my best German.

We kept them within striking distance. The one VoPo bow gunner then turned his .50-cal. to the opposite side from where it was aimed but kept his arm on the gun. More than anything, we showed them that we were not afraid of them and could care less about some imaginary boundary lines in the water. We were the Military Police and they needed to know that target practice was over.

Only Hans remained sitting down and out of sight of the VoPo guards. You could say he was a little shaken by my maneuver. I took a pack of cigarettes out of my pocket and held it up. I knew how much they valued American cigarettes.

"Comrades, cigarettes," I announced as I threw the pack to them.

The .50-cal. bow gunner let loose of his gun and caught the package in mid-air.

"Danka. Danka." (Thank you. Thank you.) He and the others replied.

Meanwhile, Rudy threw a couple of bumper guards over the starboard side to keep the boats from banging against each other. One bumper was secured to the bow cleat and the other to the stern cleat.

The highest-ranking VoPo waved at us as a gesture of good faith in exchange for the cigarettes. He then proceeded to remove the East German flag from his stern rail and threw it toward Rudy.

"Danke." (Thank you.) I responded with a head nod.

The lead VoPo then saluted in a German fashion with his palm out, and I motioned back to him. Not once did any of us take our eyes off the other. With our bow line and stern lines now being untied by the VoPo guards, I slowly inched the boat backward the way we came in.

After rounding the bend of the islet, I put us in a forward motion and gave a little more throttle. We cruised away and continued checking on all our areas of the lake. We said hello to people we didn't know and waived at the kids playing in yards. Some folks were even prepping their small boats for a beautiful day of fishing or water skiing. Other than our little challenge test with the VoPo guards, it had been a great morning.

Hans finally got out from under the counsel behind the steering wheel and looked at me like I was crazy.

"You're an insane American, Rex. We all could have gotten ourselves shot or worse." Hans exclaimed.

"Orders, Hans. Just orders to stop the VoPo guards from shooting across the lake at houses and innocent people. My orders, Hans, become your orders. Got it? We needed the element of surprise, and they were not going to shoot at a military boat that had the right to be there," I replied.

"Just warn me ahead of time, please." Hans requested.

For Hans to confront the VoPo guards was the scariest thing on earth. They were his worst nightmare and greatest problem in life. But he would never talk about why.

I asked Hans to take over at the helm and take us back to the dock for lunch. Afterward, we would head down to Bravo Checkpoint. Hans took over and gave more throttle to get back to our dock faster. Nothing more was said between us until we docked our boat.

As we docked, Rudy was smiling about what we had accomplished with the guards.

"I wonder if anyone else has ever come that close to a VoPo boat before?" Rudy inquired.

"Oh, I think so, Rudy. Today we caught them off guard, and we showed them we had no fear. They are truly confused by now and wondering what in the hell just happened." I explained.

As Hans was maneuvering our vessel backward to our dock, both Rudy and I jumped ship, each holding a tie rope and fastening them to a pier cleat. We always backed our boat in for emergency fast starts.

"Come on, guys. I will buy lunch today." I offered.

Rudy was up for that, but Hans stayed back saying he had to clean up a little and check oil, plugs, and look for any leaks.

"In case you haven't noticed, we are accumulating more water than usual in the motor compartment. I think the bilge pump is slumbering a little. I am going to see what is wrong. I will take you up on your offer next time," Hans answered.

"Ok, suit yourself. See you back on the dock within the hour," I hollered back at Hans.

Rudy and I went to our usual table closest to our office door. From our table, we could hear the phone or listen to the radio in the event of an emergency.

"What are you having today, Rudy?" I asked.

"I think a Chef's Salad. Getting tired of hamburgers all the time."

"You know, you're right, Rudy, the same hamburgers are getting old. Maddy, why don't you get me a *cheeseburger* with *bacon* on it instead today!"

"Oh, that's new and different, now isn't it?" Maddy smiled and asked with sarcasm.

"Yes, my dear, because I never have ordered one with bacon. And I would also like a tall glass of iced tea," I said.

"Me too," Rudy chimed in.

"Ok, coming right up. How is the lake today, guys?" Maddy asked.

"Beautiful," Rudy said. "Just perfect for water skiing. No wind lips on the water. Smooth as silk. You should come out with us when you get off."

Sometimes Maddy would go skiing with us. Rudy was madly in love with her. As for me, I was married to a redheaded lady. My plate was full as they say, including a baby daughter.

Rudy asked me again about the orders to roust the VoPo guards this morning.

"Was that true?" Rudy asked.

"Yeah. Capt. D mentioned the incidents hitting his desk, and he asked me if I knew anything about it? I told him I hadn't. He said to please check into it for him to find out what is going on. I did an about-face thinking he meant us to look into the VoPo guards a little."

"Sorry, Rex, but I am just a little lost here," Rudy said. "You mean he just asked you to look into it and find out what is going on? And you thought he meant for us to risk our lives sneaking up on the VoPo guards with our guns drawn? You do know how dangerous that was, don't you? I mean, hell, we could have had our heads blasted off by the .50-cal."

"I was letting them know that we know what the hell they are doing. No more, or I will keep sneaking up on them and maybe bump them overboard. I promise you there won't be any more shooting at civilians here. What I did scared the crap out of them, and rightfully so."

"Yeah, it scared the crap out of me too." Rudy said, nearly choking on the words as he spoke.

"Here you go, boys." Maddy exclaimed as she handed us our lunch. "Anything else I can get you before I take my break?"

"No, sis. I think we have all we need," I said after she slammed us about being boys, then I figured my remark was apropos.

Rudy and I were only into our second bites when we heard both the telephone and the radio going off at the same time. The words on the radio sounded all too familiar and threatening. Rudy and I both jumped up simultaneously. He answered the phone while I listened to the radio announcement.

"MP Boat 1, we need help at Bravo Checkpoint! Numerous shots fired in the canal area. We are stuck inside watching but can't see what the VoPo tower guards are shooting at."

"Bravo, this is MP-1, we are on our way. ETA 10-15 minutes. Keep me informed." I immediately answered as we rushed out the door, leaving our lunches behind. Funny how that always happens.

"Rudy, let's go, man! We've got an emergency of some sort at Bravo." I ordered.

"Yeah, that was 1st Sarg saying the same thing. He said approach with caution and find out what the hell the shooting is all about."

As I was running down the lawn toward our pier and the MP boat, I was yelling for Hans to fire her up, we had an emergency. He heard me because the engine compartment lid slammed shut, and he quickly stepped to the bridge and fired up MP-1. I scrambled to the bow cleat and untied the rope, then threw it onto the bow. More tension was placed on the stern cleat as the bow drifted a little away from the pier. As I jumped on board, over the gunnel wall, Rudy shouted that he got the other rope and threw his stern line in the back of the boat, while jumping in at the same time.

People sunbathing on the grassy lawn, others walking around, and people from inside the café were all alarmed at our departure.

As soon as I boarded MP-1, I was assisted by Hans, who grabbed my right arm and steadied me next to him as we took off at full speed. I immediately turned the blue light and siren on, indicating to all that we had an emergency. Most of the time, people anticipated a swimmer or boater in trouble. This time people were a little more alarmed after some had overheard our radio conversation inside the office area.

I remember hearing someone yell out, "Good luck out there!" as we were departing from the pier at full throttle.

"Hans, let's go!" I yelled over the roar of the engine and propeller straining at the controls being operated by him.

"Ja! I heard over the radio. Bravo Checkpoint, Ja? Shooting?" Hans said loudly.

"Yes, keep that hammer all the way down, Hans. It sounds like we are needed fast." I shouted.

I turned back to see Rudy, who was holding onto the stern balance bars.

"Get up here, Rudy!" I hollered back.

I proceeded to give Rudy instructions on what we could be facing and advising him.

"Be ready to jump in if people are in trouble or stay low with your .45 at the ready."

After saying that, the boat radio flared up with a familiar voice. It was Sgt. Johnson, the senior in command at Bravo Checkpoint, and he was announcing over the radio to us that shots were still being fired in their direction from the VoPo gun tower and he thinks a few bullets hit our outer wall.

"I don't know what the hell they are firing at, but we are ok up here. Where are you now?" Sgt. Johnson asked.

"We are turning into the Teltow Canal now and should be there in a minute or two," I reported. We continued up the canal until we got closer to the scene. A minute later I said over the radio, "Okay, Sarg, I see a small boat capsized in the water by the cattails just below you guys at Bravo Checkpoint, and one or maybe more people are in the water."

I hung the radio receiver on its hook and instructed Rudy to hand me the M14 rifle, which was next to him below the bridge.

"What is it, man, what's going on?" Rudy inquired.

"Stay down and stay quiet, Rudy. The VoPo guards are firing at something or someone in the canal up ahead."

I had just put the M14 to my shoulder and was leaning on the chrome windshield framing when the VoPo guards turned their guns directly at us. It wasn't their big tower .50-cal., but rifle fire. We took four hits on the starboard (right side) of the bow.

After that, one VoPo guard was half-sliding and half-falling as he was frantically trying to step down from the tower. Then he stopped midway, threw his rifle to the ground, and jumped the rest of the way, not even bothering to pick up his gun as he began an all-out run towards the Grunewald Forest to get away. Then it happened.

The second VoPo guard, still up in the tower, took another shot at us. This time a bullet hit the framing I was leaning on. The windshield and framing exploded in my face where I was standing. My left eye received the worst of the damage along with my head and ear from all the flying debris. I heard and felt the bullet zoom over my left ear and graze the side of my hairline. Had I been standing ½ inch to the left, I would not be here to tell this story. Glass shards were everywhere, and then I noticed that I was bleeding from the left side of my head. It felt like I was burned.

The second East German VoPo guard to
jump down from the guard tower

Not losing too much of my composure, I raised the M14 back up and placed a bullseye on the back of the first guard that was still running towards the Grunewald. I wanted him down before he reached the woods. Then I would shoot the second guard who really pissed me off for putting holes in our patrol boat and nearly killing me. Just as I was squeezing down to pull the trigger on the first guard, I heard a resounding, "*No!*"

I stopped pulling the trigger in that split-second moment. I looked left, right, and behind me. Rudy meanwhile took the opportunity to ask if he could get up and help kill something. There was no one in the boat, on the shore, or in the water that could have said "*No!*" to me. I did recognize the voice, and as I was stepping back, I took a breath and had another look as both guards were now running away to hide.

Why can't I return fire, God?

I guess I had my answer. Even though I was angry and wanted revenge, it would not be up to me today. As I put my rifle down, I was a little dazed and adrenaline weak as the two guards disappeared into the forest. I ran over to the port side of the boat, where I saw the cold-blooded carnage that the VoPo guards left behind. It was gruesome.

There were two bodies floating in the water and a capsized boat beginning to half-sink from all the bullet holes. I have no doubt that some of the holes in the boat were bullets that had passed through the man and woman.

I jumped over the side of my patrol boat and into the red water, where I experienced the bloodbath first-hand. The water was deep, so I couldn't touch the bottom. I grabbed onto the bodies before they could sink or float away and checked for any signs of life.

I made my way over to the nearest embankment on the American side at Bravo Checkpoint, pulling the bodies behind me. After wading in the water, I managed to pull each body from the water and upon the solid ground. Again, there were absolutely no signs of life, how could there be?

Never had I seen so much blood seeping out of a body so quickly. At the time, I estimated there must have been around 20 bullets that hit the victims. There was no time for CPR, tourniquets, or pressure bandages. Lives were lost, and souls were gone. We were simply too late.

The picnic basket floated in the water briefly until it sunk to the bottom of the canal. Blood splatter painted most of the nearby cattails and even the outstretched trees leaning over the water ten feet above. The scene was heart-wrenching and sickening. No longer was the water its standard green color; it was blood red. My light-colored uniform shirt was now red from all the blood. I half-stood over the two people with a gut-wrenching pain in my stomach.

Oh God, bless the souls that lay dead before me.

By this time, one of the MPs from the checkpoint came running down the hill, including Sgt. Johnson. Rudy was in the bloody water, shaking like a leaf. Fear does funny things to bodies and minds when that dark cloud of horror comes forward and smacks you in the face. It happens to everyone. I stood there for a few minutes, leaning near the bodies. Blood seeped out of the bullet holes. There was nothing I could do. It is difficult to describe the feelings inside or the looks of horror on all our faces. To this day, it is hard to grasp the scene's totality. The only true story is that both individuals died immediately from their multiple gunshot wounds. Neither of them survived because they were annihilated by the VoPo guards. I stood with their bodies for nearly 8 hours until they were taken away.

Death, bodies, and blood never bothered me before. Somehow, I coped with just about any situation or shoved it down for a second look later in life. However, this day I was speechless and stunned by the senseless horror-filled scene that was before me. How could these VoPo guards be that inhumane and ruthless as to shoot two innocent people? They opened fire to annihilate these two human beings. Many killed just for fun or to even a score. It was apparent I was still in shock.

Someone again tried to tidy up the blood running down my face, but I shook the MP off me.

"Leave me alone, I'm fine," I said. "Sarg, I need to use the phone in your office."

Sgt. Johnson yelled back, "Go ahead. Let Capt. D know what just happened. Tell him to get some help down here right away."

"OK," I yelled back as I stumbled to my feet. "Rudy, get a tarp and cover the bodies for now. Don't let anyone close to the scene except who is here right now."

"Yes, sir." Rudy acknowledged.

It took me a minute or two to reach the front door of Bravo Checkpoint. Another MP, Cpl. Dolan was anxiously awaiting news on what had happened below. He saw me covered in blood, and I could see the look of horror on his face.

"Hang on, Dolan. I've got to call Capt. D immediately." I reassured him.

Picking up the phone, I noticed my hand was shaking a little, and I was also having trouble breathing now. My knees were so weak, they felt like just giving in to whatever was overcoming me and falling to the ground. I fought to stay standing and realized I was in a state of shock. It was all catching up to me as it started to settle in.

After dialing the commander's office, I heard Capt. D's secretary ask me for my name and business. I was not in a state-of-mind for politeness.

"This is MP-1, I need to speak to Capt. D right now, we have a dire emergency!"

Lt. Jameson immediately got on the phone while they found Capt. D.

"Rex, what is going on. What is happening out there?" Lt. Jameson, asked.

"Bad news, sir. A couple was brutally fired upon by the VoPo guards in the gun tower."

"Hang on, Rex. Here he is." Lt. Jameson said as he handed the phone to Capt. D.

"Rex, it's Capt. D here. What happened?"

I relayed to him the entire story, and that this is no longer a safe zone.

"Capt. D, both individuals are dead. I suggest you block any more cars or foot traffic from coming towards Bravo. Also, stop all inbound traffic from West Germany coming through here. This is a bad situation, sir. And I'm afraid it may get a lot worse."

"Is anyone else hurt?" Capt. D asked.

"No, sir. But we need help right away." I requested.

"Help is being called for right now. Hang in there and protect the scene," Capt. D ordered.

I proceeded to do just as he asked. Horrors of this magnitude do something different to everyone. Some take it in stride, or so they think, like me. Others start shaking uncontrollably like Rudy. Some people fall to their knees in disbelief like Hans. Others get angry, and some even get sick at the sight of so much blood. None of that comes close to the fear that unravels within your mind when, across the Teltow Canal within two or three hours of the incident, you hear the military build-up of armies and equipment set for war from inside the Grunewald. It was very distressing.

Cautioning everyone to stay alert and ordering four people to man the perimeter around the dead bodies with sidearms was a joke. I had no real idea of what was going on across the canal, but it sounded like an entire army marching to war.

Four Americans were surrounding the dead couple, one of which was me. We each had a .45 cal. sidearm. There was one M14 now in Rudy's hands. Poor Hans, our one and only skipper, was hiding in the boat. We were up against an army of Russians and East Germans. The odds didn't seem quite fair.

During the next hours, I witnessed the most intense military stand-off on both sides of the canal. I thought this could be the beginning of another war. The Russians had tanks, and one or more infantry companies. I could see all their guns pointing directly at the American side from the Grunewald.

The American side had tanks, plus a company of 6th Infantry soldiers. They were pointing all their guns across the canal toward the Russians. My little troop was in the middle, with all the guns seemingly aimed at us. The tension was gripping and very intense as we stood between the growing conflict. Fear hung in the balance for everyone. It became very quiet, and everyone was at the ready. Had one person from either side fired a shot, a war would have exploded. And that is not an exaggeration – we were on the brink of war at that moment on June 15, 1965.

Rudy, Hans, the Bravo MP's, and I were in the middle at the Teltow Canal water's edge in our bullet-riddled patrol boat. I remember thinking to myself how small I really was in this world compared to the two military superpowers facing off against one another at that moment.

Thinking back, while I was aiming at the East German guard who had jumped down from the tower and was running to hide, I was ever so slowly squeezing down on the trigger intending to kill him. I alone may have started a war if I had pulled the trigger. I've had to live with the enormity of that incident all my life, and I'm forever grateful that God intervened. What if I had shot the guards? I can tell you that it would not have been good.

I knew the mere sound of one tank firing a cannonball toward Bravo Checkpoint would have taken it off the map, instantly. All that would be left is a lot of smoke where it had once stood.

We were right there amid the devastation, between the vast metal killing machines. The army personnel on both sides were at the ready. There were machine guns, nearby fighting helicopters ready and waiting, as well as jet fighters on alert and ready for take-off a few miles away in Berlin.

Soon every American Post in Germany was on high alert while the convoys of military personnel and weaponry deployed toward Bravo Checkpoint. As it turns out, the powers that be thought Bravo Checkpoint was under attack; all hell was going to break loose. This was very serious.

There was no place to hide but one. Then it came to me like a lightning bolt, *pray. Start praying for peace to return, and no further military action required. Pray for courage and strength at this moment.*

Pvt. Rudy, MP Boat Commander Rex and helmsman Hans on patrol days later.

Now I know how King David must have felt as a young man going up against his foe, the Giant Philistine Goliath (1 Samuel 17). David's battleground was at the Valley of Elah. Mine was at the Bravo Checkpoint. The difference, I didn't have to kill anyone. I could have, maybe I should have. But I heard, *No!*

Hermann Dobler's memorial on the Bravo Checkpoint embankment

The escalation of a sizable military presence continued. The next day someone showed me an East German newspaper with a headline about the incident and a picture of me half-standing over the corpses. Then I read the headline which reported something to this effect: *Now you see what the Americans do to our West-Berlin families.* I couldn't believe it, and yet I could. It was part of the culture. I wish I had a copy of that East German newspaper and picture of me with the bodies, but I cannot locate it. This newspaper had the audacity to print lies and make false accusations. The news reports had lied, and those lies perpetuated for months and years.

Over the next several days, the military standoff remained. Very slowly, through the efforts on both sides, did the political conversations de-escalate the possible war. Weeks later, the calmness of Wannsee Lake took back its beauty and serenity. MP-1 returned to normal routines and border patrols. Looking back, I thank God the potential war standoff ended before more innocent people lost their lives.

After Bravo Checkpoint

When I left Berlin and the 287th Military Police Division in 1967, I left a lot of strong memories of both good things and bad.

Looking back, I remember there was a total of seven young men, including myself and Rudy, who tested and passed pre-school flight exams. The Vietnam War seemed to be screaming our names. Now's the time, young men, to fight for your country. I guess we all yearned to go where there was real action.

A Captain from the Arizona Chopper school showed up one day in the 287th Military Police lunchroom. He looked at his new cadets, standing at attention before him and our company commander, Capt. D. His eyes looked squarely at each one of us. Then he looked at me and raised not only his head but his eyebrow as well.

"What in the hell are you doing here, young man? I know you passed all your exams with flying colors, but you would never fit in one of my birds! Sorry, but you never should have made it this far. Please leave this assembly." the Captain ordered.

I was perplexed and even hurt, from being turned away because I was too tall. I gathered up my courage and strength as I saluted the visiting Captain, then made a snappy left turn and immediately left the lunchroom. Once outside, all I could do was hang my head in disappointment, I would not be joining my friends for a more significant fight in a place called Vietnam. For me, the answer was to stay.

Capt. D and I were good friends. He and I shared a passion for race cars, and we took pleasure during the sports car racing months to race all over Europe. He had a newer Alfa Romeo, and I had an older, tired Porsche 356 that I charged up every weekend race day.

My racing days nearly ended one weekend on a German racetrack, when out of my right eye, I spotted a lone wheel quickly passing me by. Then I heard the sudden grinding noise as my right rear wheel rim dug into the pavement, leaving a rather large scar on the track. I stopped rather suddenly and unintentionally as I watched my tire roll toward the finish line. It took me a few months to put all the pieces of my car back together again. Then time itself was racing in another direction.

Six months after being denied going to chopper school, Capt. D. called me into his office.

"Rex, please sit down. There is something I need to tell you."

"What is it, Capt.?" I inquired.

As I sat, his eyes remained fixed on the piece of paper lying on the desk in front of him. I sensed that he was struggling to get the words out.

"I am sorry to tell you this. All six of your friends were shot down in Vietnam. One soldier, Eddie, is returning alive but without his legs. One of the first to be shot down was Rudy, and the others went within a month. Rex, it was good that you were denied going to Vietnam. They are turning pilots out far too soon without enough training time. The business of turning out flyboys more quickly is not right, and it should have never happened. Listen to me Rex, by the grace of God, you and I still have a job to do and races to race."

I couldn't believe it.

Epilogue: Looking Back

The worst memories, by far, were the deliberate killings of Hermann Dobler and Elke Martens. I'm not even sure Elke Martens is her real name. I've been unable to find much information about her. Hermann Dobler is being honored in several ways, but what about Elke? What happened to Elke Martens' body, and where is her grave or marker? She mattered too, yet she has disappeared.

The Berlin Wall Memorial lists Hermann Dobler as a fatality in 1965, but not Elke Martens. Interestingly though, there is one death in 1965 listed as an "Unidentified Fugitive." Maybe it is her. She deserves to have her truth be told. Maybe one day we will get to the bottom of it.

The only redeeming fact I learned in my research was that one of the VoPo guards responsible for the barbaric murders was later arrested in 1993. The shooter was tried for Murder 1. He was convicted of the killings and sentenced to 4 years in prison for murdering two innocent people.

In my opinion, justice was not served. Once again, communism played out. Maybe some of the VoPo guards' court records have information regarding Elke Martens. I know she was a young woman with blond hair who was wearing a dress that day and didn't deserve to die the way she did, so I'll be her voice too. A piece of paper was found in her pocket with the name Elke M. written on it. Nobody has any information about it. Lots of guessing, but no answers.

The second guard involved in the murders served no time and, presumably, no punishment at all. I read where the commander in charge received only 6 years of probation for giving the order to rain down bullets on Hermann and Elke. I don't believe the couple's boat ever made it as far as the Avus bridge as reported. There wasn't any blood or disturbance that far up the canal. I can attest to the fact that they did not survive.

> To Hermann Dobler and Elke Martens,
>
> *I am so sorry that I didn't get there sooner. Perhaps I could have warned you of the Teltow Canal dangers. Maybe I could have convinced you to go a little further up Wannsee Lake and spend your picnic time at a beautiful area on the lawn of our MP Boat Patrol Headquarters.*
>
> *It means little now, in all the years since that day, but I have thought about and prayed for both of you, including your families. The same goes for all the innocent people killed at Charlie Checkpoint, Bravo Checkpoint, and across Berlin. And especially for those souls whose bodies were found in Wannsee Lake.*
>
> *May you both rest in peace.*

Many of the individuals who were there with me that day are no longer with us, like Capt. D, Hans, and Rudy. Maybe, just maybe, there are others out there who remember this incident. I'm documenting my story in hopes that it will help others to tell theirs. We must learn from history to not repeat it. Can we?

For me, it has been almost 55 years of haunting memories. Hermann Dobler and Elke Martens are gone, but they will never be forgotten.

Like so many, I had lived more life before the age of 21 years than most live in their entire lives.

May God Bless us ALL.

The Berlin Wall Trail marker

Our mission is to leave no one behind, and we
failed. Who was that woman that was shot?
Where is her memorial and who will help to
place a proper marker for Elke Martens?

The End

I don't think so…

Author's Note

It is a new year, a new decade, and a unique time in our country's history and forthcoming future.

We find ourselves with a government split in several directions, with accusations, truth, lies, threats of looming war, and evidence of assassinations to political leaders around the world.

This isn't old news. The same thing happened as far back as I can remember and further back to the Civil War and beyond.

You see, men and women have not learned how to play fair and live in peace. Why, because we, as humans, think we can do it all ourselves without a God to follow. We haven't created anything that was not already present. There is nothing new under Heaven. There is only one that can make all things right, and it's not any of us. Look up. Look to God. Even Einstein said at the end of his life, "I was wrong. There is a God."

On my TV screen, I see a massive build-up of military troops and so many more getting ready for war in the middle east again. Nothing new. But I ask you to take a good look at the faces of those young and old soldiers readying themselves for war. Look close, fake smiles, fear-laden eyes, and pre-PTSD.

Researching and telling this story has profoundly affected me, a result of the experiences I endured. Our eyes are opened wide to the horrors of this world, the hurts within ourselves, and the pains of humanity around us. There is that insidious portion of our brain that records every single event and picture as it settles in and begins to grow in weird, ugly, distorted shapes in our minds. Make no mistake, everyone who has witnessed evil, war, accidents, death, bullying, slaughter of animals and humans, just to mention a few, will and does have PTSD one way or the other. Watch out for masking, running, hyper' ism, drugs, addictions of all sorts, and so on and so forth.

Some of us can live with it for years or all our life. Does that mean we just cope better or get over it? No! PTSD takes its toll on everyone in many ways as we try to adjust, re-adjust, cover-up our lives, and cope with life's everyday problems.

Wouldn't it be nice to have people in the know to talk to, learn from, follow, begin to heal, and have as healthy a life as possible? You can. At the front of this story are phone numbers and websites to go to for help. Call and stay in touch. Write and don't be afraid to feel better. Don't stay in denial, don't shrug it off as nothing or think it will pass. It won't.

Sacred ground is a term used many times over and means different things in other cultures. In my country, the USA, we have large populations of American Indians. One sacred area for them and many other cultures is burial grounds or cemeteries, and in Egypt the ancient tombs.

To the Jewish community of World War II, don't ever forget the horrors of the Nazi concentration camps where millions died.

To me, all of life is sacred. Whether friend or foe let's talk and make living in peace the more significant issue and resolve our differences. After all, God made all of us.

Last is a little history that is found in many religions. Starting with Genesis after creation, Genesis 2:7 (Man and Woman). From that point, all humans had one language. Then in Genesis, 11:1, and following, God changed man's language, and the peoples were scattered throughout the world and were changed.

What happened? Man, once again, was attempting to be like God himself. Building a tower up to God and, in turn, God reached down and destroyed the tower and changed man forever.

Despite that, man just never got over the fact that we never learned to live in peace. We are all filled with Greed, wanting Power, wanting our Own Way. Peace be damned, Love be damned, I just Want. We can live in peace and we can learn from the truth.

Funny thing, we forget that everyone's blood is red. We are all related. Black, White, Red, Yellow, Brown – All Related! Just go back to the beginning, Genesis 1. That is how it all began.

Rex Barton

Rex's next books will be about the many standoffs
and killings at Charlie Checkpoint.

REFERENCES

Other than my memory, such as it is, most of the facts derived from this Teltow Canal incident came from German newspapers, people in the know still living in Berlin, and The Bridge Hunter's Chronicles - Berlin History bridging the past with our future.

The connection between the Teltow Canal, Bravo Checkpoint and Wannsee Lake

Google (Images, Videos, Historical Information)

Wikipedia (Lists of deaths at the Berlin Wall)

The Bridges at Checkpoint Bravo (Berlin, Germany)

https://footage-berlin.com/en/berlin-border-a-boat-trip-with-a-fatal-outcome-june-15-1965/

https://www.the-berlin-wall.com/videos/the-death-of-hermann-doebler-561/

https://bridgehunterschronicles.wordpress.com/2018/09/26/the-bridges-at-checkpoint-bravo-berlin-germany/

www.chronik-der-mauer.de/en/victims/180531/doebler-hermann

https://www.berliner-mauer-gedenkstaette.de/de/

https://flensburgerfiles.wordpress.com/

Daily News (New York, New York) 16 Jun 1965, Wed. Page 199

The Central New Jersey Home News (New Brunswick, New Jersey) 16 Jun 1965 Page 27

News Pilot (San Pedro, California) 05 Aug 1965. Thu. Page 4

Albuquerque Journal (Albuquerque, New Mexico) 16 Jun 1965. Page 40

Declassified Documents

https://www.archives.gov/files/research/foreign-policy/cold-war/berlin-wall-1962-1987/dvd/pdfs/wall_2/Teltow%20Canal.pdf

Novels By Rex Barton

FICTION

The Hawk Series:
In The Eye Of The Hawk – Book 1
In The Eye Of The Hawk – Book 2
The Mongoose Diaries – Book 3
Panga Wars – Book 4

Broken Spirit Series:
Broken Spirit – Book 1
Centerfire - Book 2

Milton Keynes UK
Ingram Content Group UK Ltd.
UKHW051025250324
439991UK00008B/1022